Life in Pictures

ABBA

Marie Clayton

Trans Atlantic Press

Björn & Benny, Agnetha & Anni-Frid...

Before becoming superstars as Abba, each member of the group had individual musical success: Benny Andersson spent time as keyboard player for The Hep Stars – the 'Swedish Beatles' – and composed many of their hits; Anni-Frid 'Frida' Lyngstad was a successful singer with several Swedish hit singles; Agnetha Fältskog was a talented singer-songwriter with a Swedish No.1 at only 17; Björn Ulvaeus had been lead singer and composer for a popular Swedish folk group. Not surprisingly the four often met at various musical events, and in 1969 the two men teamed up to produce their first album together, *Lycka* – for which Agnetha and Frida recorded some backing vocals. By this time Agnetha and Björn were a couple, as were Benny and Frida, and by 1971 the four were working regularly together on each other's recordings. Agnetha, Björn and Benny soon also began performing together, but initially Frida preferred to pursue a solo career. The first single released by the four as a group was 'People Need Love' in 1972, although not as Abba – the group's initial name was descriptive but rather a mouthful: Björn & Benny, Agnetha & Anni-Frid. They also produced their first album as a group, *Ring Ring* released in March 1973 – but all four also continued to work solo.

ABBA was an acronym based on the initial letter of each group member's name – but calling the group Abba was initially only a private joke in the recording studio, because in Sweden it was also the name of a well-known company that sold preserved seafoods. However, despite a competition in a Swedish newspaper to rename the group, the name Abba stuck and by 1974 negotiations with the other Abba had achieved permission for the group to use the same name. Even so the first album to feature the new name, *Waterloo* released in March 1974, was credited to Abba (Björn & Benny, Agnetha & Anni-Frid) to avoid any possible confusion. It was not until after winning Eurovision that the group became so well known that no further qualification of the name was necessary.

Benny and Anni-Frid, Agnetha and Björn become ABBA...

Winning at Eurovision

It was only after the single 'Ring Ring' became successful in several European countries that all four members had decided to commit themselves to being a group. They were determined to reach an international audience – which they achieved in April 1974, when Abba won the Eurovision Song Contest for Sweden with 'Waterloo'. An original composition written for the competition by Benny and Björn and Abba manager Stig Anderson, with lead vocals by Agnetha and Frida, 'Waterloo' was an unusual entry for Eurovision at that time because it was a catchy pop song in English rather than a ballad in the native language of the artist's country. It reached No.1 in nine countries and made the Top Ten in another ten; it was the only Eurovision song winner to reach the Top Ten in the United States.

ABOVE: On stage during the Eurovision contest held at The Dome in Brighton, England.

OPPOSITE: Abba in Germany in September 1975; from the left Benny and Frida, Agnetha and Björn. Agnetha and Björn had married on July 6, 1971. Benny and Frida had also been an established couple since 1969, but they did not marry until October 1978 when Abba were at the height of their fame.

ABOVE: Agnetha and Frida in matching blue and yellow cat outfits by Owe Sandström, who designed many of Abba's stage clothes. Most of the stage costumes were made in triplicate: one for the current performance, one being cleaned and one waiting at the next venue. In January 2010 an interactive exhibition, Abbaworld, opened in London with 25 rooms full of memorabilia, behind-the-scenes footage, music and costumes – including many items lent by the band members themselves. After London the exhibition moved on to Australia and then to Europe.

So long?

At first many believed that Abba would turn out to be a one-hit wonder – particularly when their second single to be released in the US, 'Honey, Honey' in April 1974, only reached No.27 on the *Billboard* Hot 100. A different song, a remix of 'Ring Ring', was released as the second single in the UK and that only managed No.32. In addition their first European tour, which began in November 1974, was initially unsuccessful with some concerts having to be cancelled due to poor ticket sales. That might have been the end of Abba, but another single, 'So Long' released in November 1974, reached the Top Ten in Sweden and Austria, while the second leg of the tour – which began in January 1975 and took Abba through the Scandinavian heartlands – was outstandingly successful with every date sold out.

Abba appearing live on *Saturday Night Live* in the US in November 1975. The group made their first visit to the United States on the back of the success of 'Waterloo' and to promote the American version of their album *Waterloo*; the trip consisted mainly of television performances and was not a tour.

Abba-mania in Australia

Continuing success with a wider international audience at first proved slightly harder to achieve. Despite being a hit in Europe 'So Long' didn't even reach the top 50 in the UK and didn't do much better in the US and Australia either. But it was followed by 'I do, I do, I do, I do, I do' in April 1975, which became Abba's next big international hit reaching No.1 in four countries and the Top Five in six more. It not only became their first Australian No.1 but also marked the very beginning of Abba-mania down-under. It even reached No.15 in the US – but only just scraped into the top 40 in Britain, mostly because it received very little airplay on influential Radio 1. However, the following single, 'SOS' first released in June 1975, did crack the British market by reaching No.6 – as well as giving Abba a second No.1 in Australia, New Zealand and South Africa.

During 1975 the single 'SOS' was the most-played song on US radio stations.

Mamma Mia

The last three singles had come from Abba's third album, *Abba* released in April 1975, and initially there were no plans to release a fourth single from the same LP. However, Australia was clamouring for more Abba and a promotional clip for the song 'Mamma Mia' was proving particularly popular so it was decided to release that as a single too. It was a good decision: 'Mamma Mia', released in September 1975, not only spent ten weeks at the top spot in Australia but also gave Abba their first No.1 in the UK singles chart.

OPPOSITE: Frida and Agnetha in November backstage in New York in 1975. By now Abba had achieved four international hit singles, plus a few hits in lesser markets but this didn't stop the group releasing their first compilation album, *Greatest Hits* in November 1975 – even though there were not yet enough genuine hit singles to make up an entire LP. Neither *Waterloo* nor *Abba* had done that well in the major album charts of the US and the UK: *Waterloo* had reached No.145 in the US and No.28 in the UK, while *Abba* had made No.174 and No.13 on the *Billboard* 200. Ironically *Greatest Hits* did better than both, finally taking the No.1 spot in the UK Album chart – and staying in the Top 40 for 72 consecutive weeks – as well as making it to No.48 in the *Billboard* 200.

International superstardom

It was in 1976 that Abba became firmly established as superstars. The *Greatest Hits* album had included 'Fernando' for some countries, a song that had originally been written for Frida in Swedish and had featured on her solo hit album, *Frida ensam* (Frida alone) in 1975. It had been outstandingly successful in Swedish, so Abba decided to record an English version, for which Björn wrote completely different lyrics. After it was released in March 1976, 'Fernando' became one of their biggest hits to date, reaching No.1 in thirteen countries and only just missing the top spot in another five. In Australia it became one of the best-selling singles of all time and although it only reached No.13 on the *Billboard* Hot 100, it made No.1 on the *Billboard* Adult Contemporary chart so became their first US No.1.

ABOVE: Björn in 1976.

The single 'Fernando' sold over 10 million copies worldwide and was Abba's first US No.1.

'Dancing Queen', the perfect combination of voice and instruments, hit the no.1 spot in 14 countries.

Dancing Queen

At the same time as 'Fernando' was being recorded Abba had also recorded 'Dancing Queen' but it had been decided to release 'Fernando' first because a ballad was a better contrast to their previous hit, 'Mamma Mia'. Rather appropriately 'Dancing Queen' was performed in public for the first time at a gala to celebrate the marriage of King Carl XVI of Sweden and Silvia Sommerlath. When it was released in August 1976 it quickly became the iconic Abba song – as well as reaching No.1 in 14 countries and in the Eurochart Hot 100.

ABOVE AND OPPOSITE: Agnetha on Dutch television in 1976, and Björn about the same period. At the time Agnetha was expecting their second child, Peter, who was born in December

Arrival – 'the classic pop album'

Success followed success; the fourth album, *Arrival* first released in Sweden in October 1976 and three months later in the US, quickly went No.1 in almost every album chart around the world. It even climbed high in the US album charts, the first Abba album to reach the Top 20 in the *Billboard* 200. Musically it has often been regarded as the classic pop album, receiving glowing reviews from respected music magazines such as *Melody Maker* and *New Musical Express*.

LEFT: Inspired by skiffle music in the 1950s, Björn asked for his first guitar aged 13. In 1963 Björn's band attracted the attention of Stig Anderson's Polar Music, who were looking for a group to sing folk songs in Swedish, rather than follow the fashion to copy British and American bands. So the West Bay Singers became the Hootenanny Singers and were the first group to sign with Polar Music. The group had a string of hits in Sweden, interrupted in 1966 by the fact that most of the members of the band were required to do their national military service. It was at a party following their farewell show in 1966 that Björn encountered Benny Andersson, who was performing with the popular Hep Stars.

OPPOSITE: Agnetha on stage. It was on a television show that she and Björn met.

Innovative videos

The next big hit to be released from *Arrival* was 'Money, Money, Money' in November 1976. The promo video for this was directed by Lasse Hallström, who had directed most of Abba's promo clips since 'Waterloo'. For 'Money, Money, Money' he was inspired by the film *Cabaret*, showing Frida in 'reality' dressed in clothes reminiscent of the 1920s intercut with a 'dream sequence' showing the good life that might be had with enough money. He said later that this video was his favourite of the work he had done with Abba: 'It was consistent with the lyrics and the music. I loved editing my films to fit the music, to emphasize the rhythm and the idea of the music, to provide musical support and not just tell a story.' One innovative effect introduced in Abba promos was their 'profile and full-face' shots, in which one singer was seen in profile in the foreground against a full face shot of the other in the background.

The Girl With The Golden Hair

Even before Abba, Benny and Björn had dreamed of writing a full-scale musical so when they were preparing for their 1977 tour they decided to put together a mini-musical to end the main show in a spectacular way. The storyline was about a girl – *The Girl With The Golden Hair* – with a talent for singing, who leaves her home town, becomes a star and then finds herself trapped by fame. Agnetha and Frida shared the role, wearing identical costumes and golden wigs to underline the fact that they were both playing the same character. The first song was an early arrangement of 'Thank You For the Music', sung by Agnetha, but with slightly different lyrics from the version that was later released as a single. Only those who attended the concerts on the 1977 tour more than 30 years ago have ever seen *The Girl With The Golden Hair* in full.

Opposite: Abba pictured in Beverly Hills circa 1976.

‘Their singles have story lines and points of view’

Fear of flying...

Opposite: One problem that affected Abba's ability to tour was that Agnetha was deeply afraid of flying. One of the concerts on the North American leg of their tour had to be re-scheduled due to her 'emotional distress' after their private plane was delayed by bad weather, as a result of which it had to circle the airport for some time until it could land.

Right: Göran Bror 'Benny' Andersson started to play the accordion at the age of six, and he always retained his love of the instrument – and of the folk music he had played with his father, Gösta and grandfather Efraim. In 1956, when he was ten, he learned the piano and by 1964 had become keyboard player with The Hep Stars. He had co-written several songs for the Melodifestivalen – the Swedish finals to decide their entry for Eurovision – before the breakthrough with 'Waterloo', which he co-wrote with Björn. In 2002 he was awarded an honorary doctorate by the University of Stockholm for services to music, so is now officially Dr Andersson.

Almost without exception, Abba only performed songs that they had written themselves – the one exception was a cover of several folk songs on the B-side of 'Summer Night City', released in September 1978. In 1975, ABBA had been approached to contribute to an album *Stars Im Zeichen Eines Guten Sterns* (Artists In The Sign Of A Good Star), a West German charity album in aid of the battle against cancer. All participating artists were asked to record medleys of folk songs in the public domain as far as copyright was concerned, so that none of the proceeds would be lost to song-writing royalties. Abba chose American folk tunes: 'Pick A Bale Of Cotton', 'On Top Of Old Smokey' and 'Midnight Special' – Björn had started his career in music as a member of the Hootenanny Singers, who had played nothing but American folk music.

ABB

Abba on tour

Unlike many bands of their stature, Abba were reluctant to tour. This was partly because all four members had been on tour during their careers before Abba so they knew about the realities of weeks away from home; Agnetha and Björn had young children during the Abba years and were reluctant to be away from them for long periods. But another reason was that the two men thought touring was a waste of time – it was much more productive to spend that time writing and recording to craft the perfect song. It was only really Frida who preferred to be on stage in front of an audience. However, in January 1977 Abba began a short tour of Europe and Australia – and in Australia they were greeted with mass hysteria throughout the entire two-week run; fans lined the streets whenever they arrived in a new city, the media besieged them nearly 24/7. Agnetha, in particular, said later that she never really came to terms with the experience of being surrounded by fan hysteria.

LEFT AND ABOVE: Abba perform in the *Midnight Special* in Los Angeles, February 4, 1977.

Divorce...

In January 1979, after nearly eight years of marriage, Agnetha and Björn had announced they were divorcing. The news immediately caused fears that Abba would also split, although they assured fans that their personal problems would not affect the band. The break-up did inspire Björn to write 'The Winner Takes It All'; although he has pointed out that most of the song is pure fiction, he has also admitted that its narrative – dealing with a couple going their separate ways and the heartbreak that inevitably follows – had its roots in his and Agnetha's separation, 18 months previously. It seemed inevitable that Agnetha would be the lead vocalist on this song and she herself has often singled out 'The Winner Takes It All' as her favourite from the ABBA years. 'The lyrics are deeply personal, and the music is unsurpassed. Singing it was like acting a part. I mustn't let my feelings take over. It was quite a while afterwards before I realized that we'd made a small masterpiece.'

OPPOSITE AND ABOVE: In London at the Wembley Arena in November 1979.

A record for UNICEF

On January 9, 1979, a special benefit concert was held in the United Nations General Assembly in New York City to raise money for UNICEF world hunger programmes, and to mark the beginning of the International Year Of The Child. Each of the participating artists contributed a special song, donating the royalties for that song to UNICEF. Abba's contribution was 'Chiquitita', which was subsequently released on January 16 and became another big hit; the song was recently estimated to have earned UNICEF more than £1 million. Here they are pictured in rehearsal.

In September 1979 Abba set out on a tour of North America and Europe, with six nights spent at London's Wembley Arena, where a television special, *ABBA In Concert* was filmed. As it turned out, *ABBA In Concert* and *ABBA – The Movie* were to become the only record of the group live in their heyday in a bona fide arena concert.

ABOVE: Frida and Agnetha perform at the UNICEF Gala in New York in January 1979. Other artists on the bill included The Bee Gees, John Denver, Earth, Wind and Fire and Rod Stewart.

OPPOSITE: Abba appear on the *Mike Yarwood Christmas Show* at BBC Television Centre in London in December 1978.

LEFT AND OPPOSITE: Performing in at Wembley Arena London, November 9 1979. The official Abba logo had the first B backwards, a motif that was invented by Rune Söderqvist – the designer for many of Abba's album covers – in 1976. His idea was that, since they were two couples at the time, each B should look towards an A.

Anni-Frid Synni Lyngstad, better known as Frida, was born in Norway – her mother was Norwegian and her father was German – but her mother soon moved to Sweden and Frida grew up there. She made her stage debut at 11 and by 13 was working as a vocalist with a band. After Abba she continued with her solo career, but also became involved with charity work. In 1992 she married Prince Heinrich Ruzzo Reuss of Plauen; her official title is Her Serene Highness Princess Anni-Frid Synni Reuss, Countess of Plauen.

BA

Voulez Vous was the first Abba album to be recorded at Abba's own Polar Studios in Stockholm. Since then many famous artists including Led Zeppelin, Genesis and Celine Dion have recorded there.

Voulez-vous?

Abba's sixth album *Voulez-Vous*, recorded between March 1978 and March 1979, had been released in April 1979. At the time disco music was particularly popular – a theme that runs through the album. It reached No.1 in 12 countries, including the UK, and provided several hit singles, including 'Does Your Mother Know', and the title track, 'Voulez-Vous'. However, a much bigger hit was 'Gimme! Gimme! Gimme! (A Man After Midnight)', released in October 1979, which hit the top spot in five countries and the Top Ten in six more.

The beginning of the end...

In 1981 Benny and Frida announced that they were also to divorce, and Björn married Lena Kallersjo. Although they were still discussing recordings the will to continue as Abba was beginning to fail and December 1982 saw the group's last performance, which was filmed in a studio in Stockholm and transmitted live to the UK. The following year Björn and Benny were working on *Chess* with Tim Rice, while both Agnetha and Frida were concentrating on their respective solo careers. However, the end of Abba was never officially announced and for a year or so afterwards all the band members denied that they had split and hinted that there were working on a new album. It was not to appear.

Mamma Mia! the musical has been seen by more than 42 million people.

Abba goes on...

But this wasn't the end of Abba. Despite not being together any more the group continued to sell millions of records – particularly after songs were used in the soundtracks of the hit movies *Muriel's Wedding* and *Priscilla, Queen of the Desert*. In 1999 London saw the première of the hugely successful musical *Mamma Mia!*, based on the songs of Abba. The musical opened on Broadway two years later, and today it is the world's most popular show, having been seen by more than 42 million people. The fifth anniversary of the musical *Mamma Mia!* in London in 2004 was attended by Björn, Benny and Frida, while the première in Abba's home country of Sweden in February 2005 was attended by all four members of the group.

ABOVE AND OPPOSITE: Abba pictured in Paris circa 1980.

Thank you for the music...

A hugely successful movie version of *Mamma Mia!*, starring Meryl Streep and Pierce Brosnan, opened in July 2008 – the Stockholm première was also attended by all four Abba members. However, in an interview with the *Sunday Telegraph* in July 2008, Björn said there was nothing that could entice them back on stage. 'We will never appear on stage again. There is simply no motivation to re-group. Money is not a factor and we would like people to remember us as we were: young, exuberant, full of energy and ambition.'

This is a Transatlantic Press book
First published in 2012

Transatlantic Press
38 Copthorne Road
Croxley Green, Hertfordshire
WD3 4AQ, UK

A catalogue record for this book is available from the British Library.

ISBN 978-1-908533-94-4

Printed in China